SNOWPLOWS

by Jeffrey Zuehlke

PULL AHEAD BOOKS
Mighty Movers

Lerner Publications Company • Minneapolis

Dedicated to Old Man Winter

Lerner Publications Company
A division of Lerner Publishing Group
241 First Avenue North
Minneapolis, MN 55401 U.S.A.

Website address: www.lernerbooks.com

Words in **bold type** are explained in a glossary on page 30.

Library of Congress Cataloging-in-Publication Data

Zuehlke, Jeffrey, 1968–
    Snowplows / by Jeffrey Zuehlke.
        p.   cm.
    Includes index.
    ISBN-13: 978-0-8225-6009-8 (lib. bdg. : alk. paper)
    ISBN-10: 0-8225-6009-7 (lib. bdg. : alk. paper)
    1. Snowplows—Juvenile literature. 2. Snow removal—
Juvenile literature. I. Title.
    TD868.Z84 2007
    625.7'63–dc22   2005032889

Manufactured in the United States of America
1 2 3 4 5 6 – JR – 12 11 10 09 08 07

Whoa! Look at all the snow! How will these cars get home?

Here comes a snowplow! A snowplow is a truck with a plow in front.

Snowplows clear streets. They move snow so cars can get through.

Snowplows come in different sizes.
This big plow is hooked up to a
dump truck.

This smaller plow is on a pickup truck.

Small snowplows do the small jobs.
They clear driveways and parking lots.

Big snowplows do the big jobs. They clear streets and highways.

Big snowplows have powerful engines.
Engines make snowplows run. They help
snowplows push lots of heavy snow.

Snowplows also have big, thick tires.
The big tires grip the icy streets.

Most big trucks have two plows. This plow is called the **front plow**. The front plow moves most of the snow.

The **underbelly plow** clears the rest.
It is on the bottom of a snowplow.

This is called the **rub iron**. The rub iron scrapes against the curb. It keeps the plow from getting damaged by the hard curb.

The bottom of the plow is called the
cutting edge. It rubs against the
ground. The cutting edge protects the
plow from the hard street or highway.

Most plows are shaped like the letter C.

The bottom part scrapes the snow up.
The snow slides up the plow. Then it
curls around to the side.

The snowplow leaves the snow on the side of the road.

The **lift frame** connects the plow to
the truck. The lift frame lifts and lowers
the plow. The plow stays off the
ground when it isn't pushing snow.

The plow controls move the plow up
and down. But who uses the controls?

The snowplow **operator**! The operator drives the snowplow.

The operator sits in the cab. The cab
is warm and dry.

Did you know that some snowplows do more than just move snow? This truck is carrying sand and salt.

The **spreader** sprinkles sand and salt on the road.

The salt melts snow and ice. The sand
makes the road less slippery.

The street is all clear!

This snowplow is heading home. It will be ready for the next snowstorm!

Facts about Snowplows

- Snowplows clear millions of miles of streets and highways each winter.

- Snowplows spread millions of tons of salt each year. In Minnesota alone, snowplows spread more than 230,000 tons of salt in one winter season.

- Before a big snowstorm, snowplows spread a mixture of salt and water on the streets. The mixture keeps ice from forming on the streets.

- A snowplow fully loaded with sand and salt can weigh as much as seventeen cars.

- Some front plows are as wide as twelve feet. That's wider than two couches!

Parts of a Snowplow

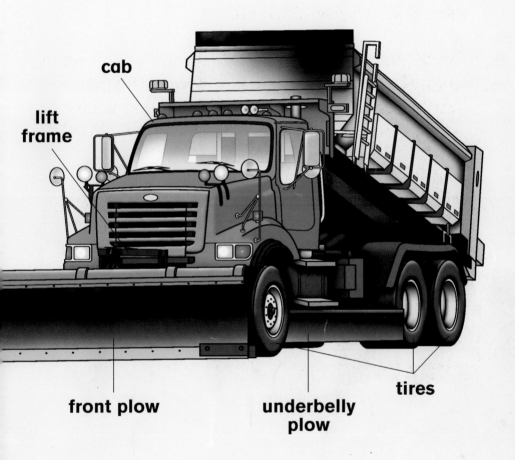

cab

lift frame

front plow

underbelly plow

tires

Glossary

cutting edge: the bottom part of a plow that rubs against the street or pavement

front plow: a large plow on the front of a truck

lift frame: a machine that connects the plow to the truck. The lift frame also lifts the plow up and down.

operator: a person who drives a snowplow

rub iron: a piece of metal on the side of a plow. It keeps the plow from hitting the curb.

spreader: a machine that sprinkles sand, salt, or a sand and salt mixture onto the road

underbelly plow: a plow on the underside of a truck

More about Snowplows

Check out these books and websites to find out more about snowplows.

Books

Glaser, Linda. *It's Winter!* Minneapolis: Millbrook Press, Inc., 2002.
  Check out this book to learn more about the winter season.

Jango-Cohen, Judith. *Dump Trucks.* Minneapolis: Lerner
  Publications Company, 2003.
  This book explains how big trucks work.

Rogers, Hal. *Snowplows.* Chanhassen, MN: The Child's
  World, 2001.
  Full-color photographs bring snowplows to life in this book.

Websites

Kids Construction Zone
  http://www.dot.state.mn.us/kids/construction/
  View photographs of snowplows and read winter fun facts on
  this website from the Minnesota Department of Transportation.

Winter Storms
  http://www.fema.gov/kids/wntstrm.htm
  This website from the United States government has games
  and information about staying safe in winter weather.

Index

Photo Acknowledgments

The photographs in this book appear with the permission of: © Richard Hamilton Smith/CORBIS, front cover; Minnesota Department of Transportation/David Gonzalez, pp. 3, 4, 5, 6, 9, 10, 11, 12, 13, 14, 15, 16, 17, 18, 19, 20, 21, 22, 23, 24, 25, 26, 27; © The BOSS Snowplow, pp. 7, 8. Illustration on p. 29 © Laura Westlund/Independent Picture Service.